THE MUSIC ROAD

A Journey in Music Reading

by Constance Starr

Book 2

> "Start out with the easiest matter; let the children master this simplest thing before advancing further; then, gradually add a little at a time to this perfectly mastered matter."
>
> Pestalozzi (1746-1827)
> Famous Swiss Educator

Cover Design and Illustrations by William Starr, Jr.

Copyright © 1981 by Summy-Birchard Music
division of Summy-Birchard Inc.
All Rights Reserved
Printed in USA

ISBN: 087487-611-7
Library of Congress Catalog Card
#85-050890

Summy-Birchard Inc.
exclusively distributed by Alfred Music

Sight-reading - A Valuable Skill

2

Teachers and Parents, Please Read BEFORE beginning the Music Road

"While good sight-reading is obviously essential to a would-be professional musician, it is no less important to the amateur. Maintaining or dropping an interest in music as a hobby will depend in almost exact proportion to the student's ability to read at sight. If there is nothing to play but the pieces learned in earlier days of study and no time to practice new ones, interest will soon die, whereas the good reader may keep interest alive with almost unlimited new material. I would therefore remind teachers (and parents) that sight-reading is NOT an optional side-line but a valuable skill for every music student."

Sir Ernest MacMillan,
Canadian Author and Music Educator

What is the difference between "reading" music and "sight-reading" music?

Recognizing and understanding musical symbols by name and definition without placing them in time and tempo is often called "reading" music. It is basically "working-out" reading. It requires time for consideration and study. This is the kind of reading used by the traditional student to learn new repertoire.

In "sight-reading" music, the reader, after scanning the printed page for important information, i.e., key signature, time signature, tempo indication, etc., gives an 'on-the-spot,' reasonably accurate musical performance. She is sight-reading the music.

Sight-reading is considered a complex psycho-motor skill, but a valuable one that ensures a lifetime of enjoyment for those who develop it.

———————

I consider myself very fortunate. I had the opportunity to become a competent, confident keyboard sight-reader at an early age. Because of that ability I enjoyed many wonderful musical experiences.

Naturally, I wanted to give my Suzuki students that same gift. I wanted to find the best way to present this skill to young students, so I began to study the research available on keyboard music reading.

You can imagine my excitement when I learned that the conclusions of the research were in direct agreement with the Suzuki way of teaching young students.

———————

The important research conclusions are listed in the next column.

Optimal Visibility Is Essential to Learning at Early Age Levels

If musical symbols are BIG and SIMPLE, it is possible, with training and practice, for the immature visual system to accomplish the complex skill of music reading at an early age.

Slow Rate of Progress Is Necessary and Normal in Early Sensory-Motor Learning

A great number of experiences are needed for the child to absorb newly learned material. Repeated sensory experiences of seeing, writing, playing, feeling, and listening at each step of learning fulfills that need.

Retention of learned material is important for beginning readers. If there are not enough repeated experiences with newly learned material, it will not be retained or remembered.

Overlearning and review are the means for retention and remembering.

Automatic response is the final desired result. A task must be done until it is ridiculously simple and the response is automatic, without necessary thought. Then, and only then, is it time for the young child to progress to the next learning step.

Early successes are important to beginners' motivation . All of the above observations support early successes at each beginning step.

Functional Definitions of musical symbols are important.
"What does it sound like? How does it feel? How long does it last?"
Hands on experience, seeing, feeling, and hearing what the symbols tell us is more than important, it is necessary sensory information for effective learning.

———————

"Sight-reading a musical score and playing it on an instrument requires precise coordination of many brain and muscle operations," reports a study of the brain activity involved in sight-reading music.
Dr. Justine Sergent, a neuroscientist writes, "It is hard to think of any other human activity (than sight-reading) that calls for the implementation of so many processes for their immediate realization."*

———————

Now that you are convinced of the complexity of this task and know what is necessary for a young reader's success, you will better understand the progression of material presented in the MUSIC ROAD. You will see that all of the above needs are recognized and developed to provide the most favorable learning environment possible. You will recognize, too, that Suzuki's philosophy and method follow these research findings closely, and why, subsequently, Suzuki students benefit greatly from this presentation.

———————

* "Trends in Neurosciences," May, 1993.

Practical Practice Points
for
Teachers and Parents

Stop! Look! Play!—Destinations

The playing experiences provided in these two sections explore the material learned in the preceding learning section. The importance of repeated playings of these examples and pieces cannot be overestimated. Only by repetition can the desired visual-motor development occur that is the skill of sight-reading. It is advisable that the musical examples be played in different order as they are repeated so that recognition is not dependent upon sequence of sound or location.

1) Keep Eyes on Music

If the student was impressed with the importance of keeping his eyes on the music as he played in Book I, he should now have established this habit. Only the student who mentally "sees" and "feels" the keyboard while keeping his eyes on the musical notation can expect to become a competent reader.

It is absolutely necessary that the student continues to keep his eyes on the music during all repeated playings. A student who sees music symbols and patterns and experiences the motor responses to them again and again will develop the automatic response required for sight-reading. Musicians play at sight easily when their stockpile of musical memories triggers instantaneous mental and motor responses.

2) Count and "Feel" Rhythmic Meter

Notice that no 'counting aloud' is expected during playing. The student should be instructed to establish the tempo and meter by counting one measure aloud before playing. The vocal counting should be 'staccato' with obvious accents on the strong beats, as 1 2, 1 2 3, 1 2 3 4, 1 2 3 4 5 6, etc. The meter needs to be felt by the student and become obvious in his playing, by slight accents on strong beats.

It is helpful for the student to continue to "feel" beats of held notes (whole, half, dotted half, and now, dotted quarter). With the addition of the dotted quarter note this "silent" beat should also be felt by a slight beat of the arm. Most instrumentalists experience physical involvement during duration of sound (drawing a bow across the strings, blowing into a brass or woodwind instrument). If the keyboard student is encouraged to use a slight but definite arm beat on held notes, pulse and duration can be felt. This will be discarded as experience grows, leaving no detrimental after-effects ('pumping' the arm, etc.) in the playing.

3) Tempo

Just as in beginning language reading a child stops to sound out words, the beginning music reader should "stop" and "feel" intervals instead of plunging ahead impulsively to stay in time.

In subsequent readings, he can assume a steady tempo, but a slow one, slow enough to allow for necessary thought and direction but still having a rhythmic flow. If the tempo is a fraction too fast too soon, it can cause confusion when even simple one hand melodies are played.
Suggested beginning tempo: ♩ = MM 48.

4) Fingering

Fingering is indicated only when considered necessary. Since five finger positions are used exclusively in Books I and II, the student is expected to develop a "picture" and "feel" for the keyboard location of each position and each note within that position. This eliminates the possibility of reading fingering instead of spatial interval relationships.

Here is a helpful exercise:

Ask the student to put RH in treble C position, or RH or LH in middle C position, then close his eyes. Now name a note, C,D,E,F, or G, and ask the student to play it. To do this the student must mentally picture the notes on the keyboard and the location of the fingers. Do this in all positions.

5) Accompaniments

Accompaniments are provided for most of the one line musical examples and pieces. During the first few playings of any of these examples it is best to refrain from using the accompaniments because the student should be free from the pressure of staying "in time." As mentioned above under "Tempo", the student should be allowed to "picture" and "feel" the location of notes and be free to find his way without the pressure of the rhythmic framework. When the music is played with some rhythmic flow and accuracy, the accompaniments may be used profitably.

The accompaniments fill two needs: 1) They provide a rhythmic and harmonic structure against which the student can recognize errors and check himself. The accompaniments should be played with audible rhythmic accent for this reason. 2) The accompaniments provide a more 'complete' sound similar to duet playing which makes repeated playings pleasurable. The companionship of the teacher or parent in the joint venture is an added bonus!

6) Evaluation by Teacher or Parent

Evaluative comments by the teacher or parent following the first playing of any musical example should be encouraging and supportive. If incorrect notes were played, the teacher or parent may say:

"You played some notes that were different from those written. When you play it again you will probably get all of it."

If, after two or three playings, corrections have still not been made, the teacher or parent may narrow the possibilities:

"The different notes you played are in the last line."

"You should look at the second measure."

"What is the name of this note?"

"Is this interval a second or a third?"

It is best to help the student find his own errors, instead of telling him what they are. In this way he is made to think and learn from his mistakes.

Unit One · Page 6

The use of different syllables in counting the second half of each beat identifies the beat to which that half beat belongs, thereby placing it in a definite spot in the measure. It is not just **any** half beat, it is the half beat of 2 or 4, etc. Before the student uses the counting system on pages 6 and 7, he should practice saying "one-na, two-ta, three-ra, four-fa", until he can say it rapidly without stumbling. This can be approached as a 'tongue-twister'!

Unit One · Pages 6, 7, 8

At first, counting the half beats is necessary for understanding the placement of the eighth notes within the rhythmic structure; however, counting divided beats must be discarded as soon as this understanding takes place. If the student is to become an able reader, he must 'feel', without counting, the placement of the eighth note and the dotted quarter and eighth within the rhythmic structure.

Unit One · Page 8, "Return to Page 7"

The student should be instructed to 'feel', with a slight beat of the arm, the 'silent' beat during the held quarter note.

Unit Two · Page 22

At first, counting each beat in 6/8 time is necessary for understanding the place of the eighth notes within the rhythmic structure; however, since most music in 6/8 time is felt in two beats, this should be discarded as soon as possible. The student must "feel" the three eighth notes to each beat without counting them separately.

Unit Four · Page 54

(The half step is introduced here as a ♯ or ♭ . Since the interval of a second was introduced in Book I as being on a consecutive line and space on the staff and consecutive keys on the keyboard, the use of the words "whole step" or explanation of major and minor seconds should be deferred until the introduction of keys and scales in Book III.)

The student's attention should be directed to the fingering in these musical examples.

Here is a helpful exercise:

Put RH in C position. Play C D C C♯ (1 2 1 2), D E D D♯ (2 3 2 3), Play G F G G♭ (5 4 5 4), E D E E♭, (3 2 3 2) etc. LH should be done also.

In musical example 4 the flats are played with different fingers because of the melodic line.

Here is another exercise:

Put RH in C position. Play C E E♭ E (1 3 2 3), E G G♭G (3 5 4 5) Do with LH also.

Unit Four · Page 56

In the musical examples using rests the student's attention should be called to the fact that although his part is silent the accompaniment is providing the beat or half beats during that silence.

Stop! Look! Play Destinations

In all Stop! Look! Play! sections and in all Destinations, the student should prepare by naming the clef, time signature, hand, note and finger, and count one measure at performance tempo.

Suggested beginning tempo: ♩ =MM 48.

Counting should be 'staccato', stressing strong beats.

Student should not feel 'pushed' during his first efforts. Accompaniments should be used only after the third or fourth playing, and should always be played with strong rhythmic accents.

There must be much repetition of the musical examples and pieces in these sections. If the student keeps his eyes on the music during the repeated playings, he will find that the psycho-motor connections are being reinforced and will be recognized when seen in a different context.

Two suggestions to help break any possible dependence on sequence of sound or location are: 1) playing the examples in varied order on the page 2) working through the pages backwards.

"Checks" on Destinations

1. Point to individual notes. Student tells name of note and plays it.
2. Point to individual measures. Student recites names of notes, then plays the measure.

Give the student sufficient experience with each destination before going on to the next unit. If the playing has a consistent flow and there is an immediate response to the checks listed above, the student is ready to move to new material.

Home Assignments

All of the written Home Assignments in each unit should be repeated often enough to allow sufficient mental absorption and retention.

The teacher should encourage the student to write his assignments neatly and legibly since he must play what he has written. A few instructions are given on the inside of the Music Sheets folder. Additional suggestions are:

1) Intervals should be written melodically and be set off by bar lines.
2) Each four-measure musical example should be on a separate line, and should end on the first note of the position it represents, i.e., the last note in C position should be C, the last note in G position should be G.
3) The student should write the page number and the date on each assignment to facilitate the teacher's checking the assignment.

CONTENTS

UNIT ONE

Stop! Look! Learn!

INTERVAL
of a
4TH

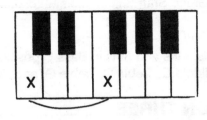

On the keyboard a 4TH looks like this.
Two keys are skipped.

On the staff a 4TH looks like this. One line and one space are skipped.

LINE	SPACE
SPACE	LINE

4TH UP　　　　　　　　　4TH DOWN

Put an X on the key a 4TH ABOVE each named key.
Connect the 2 keys.

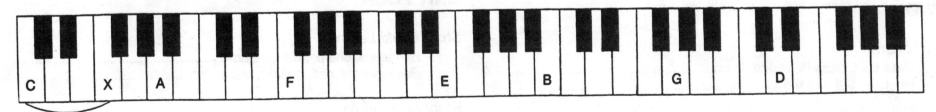

Draw a note on the line or space a 4TH ABOVE each note.

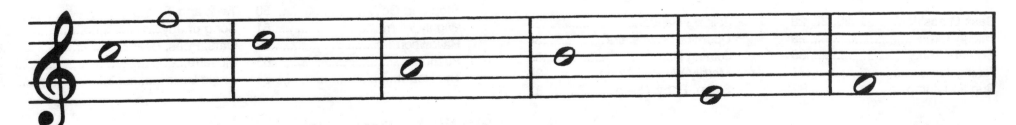

Put an X on the key a 4TH BELOW each named key.   Connect the 2 keys.

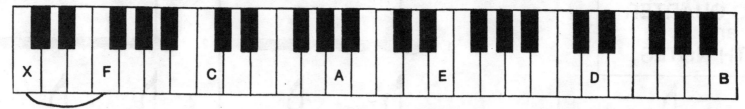

Draw a note on the line or space a 4TH BELOW each note.

Connect and mark all the 4THS.

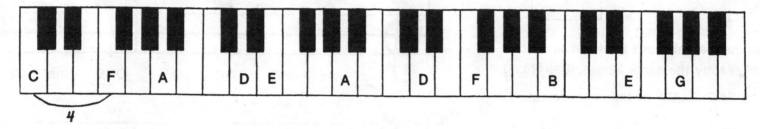

Connect and mark all the 4THS.

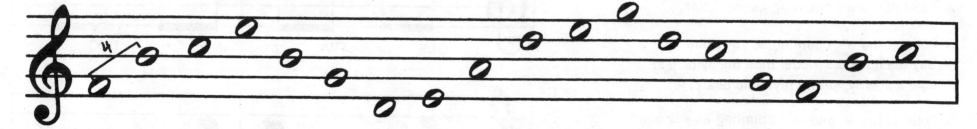

Daily Home Assignment: On the staff draw a treble clef and the treble notes C, D, E, F, G. Then draw the notes a 4th <u>BELOW</u> each one. Now, again draw treble notes C, D, E, F, G on the staff but draw the notes a 4th <u>ABOVE</u> each one. Name and <u>play the notes</u>.

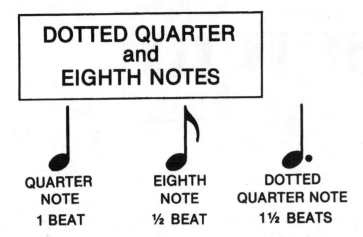

QUARTER NOTE — 1 BEAT

EIGHTH NOTE — ½ BEAT

DOTTED QUARTER NOTE — 1½ BEATS

Anything divided in half is cut into 2 parts of exactly the same size.

½ ½   ½ ½

The sound of a note that lasts one beat can be divided into 2 sounds of exactly the same length. (See No. 1)

Notes played on EACH HALF of the beat are called EIGHTH NOTES.

Count them this way: 1 na 2 ta 3 ra 4 fa

A. Point at the ♩ , counting as you point.

B. Point at the ♪ , counting as you point.
   Say the numbers louder than the syllables.
   Feel a steady, strong rhythmic beat!

C. Point at the ♩. and ♪ counting as you point.
   You will hear that the ♪ is on "ta",
   the second half of the second beat.

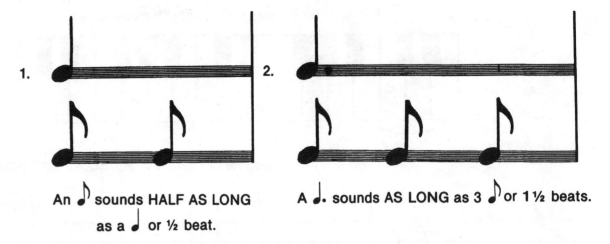

1. An ♪ sounds HALF AS LONG as a ♩ or ½ beat.

2. A ♩. sounds AS LONG as 3 ♪ or 1½ beats.

Eighth notes may have separate flags (♪ ♪) or connecting beams (♫). The beams usually appear in keyboard music.

A.
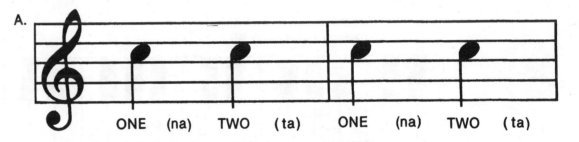

ONE (na) TWO (ta) ONE (na) TWO (ta)

B.
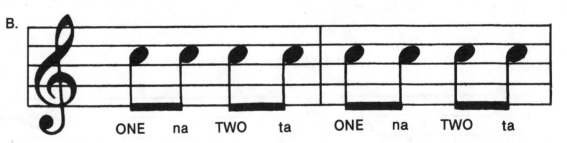

ONE na TWO ta ONE na TWO ta

C.
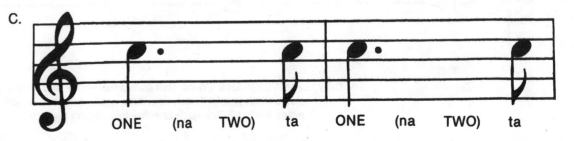

ONE (na TWO) ta ONE (na TWO) ta

1. Draw a line under each HALF beat.

2. Point and count: 2/4 1 na 2 ta.   3/4 1 na 2 ta 3 ra.   4/4 1 na 2 ta 3 ra 4 fa.

1.

1 na 2 ta

2.

1 na 2 ta 3 ra

3.

1 na 2 ta 3 ra 4 fa

4.

Daily Home Assignment: On the staff draw a treble clef. Write a 4 measure rhythmical sequence on treble C in 2/4 time using ♩,♩. and ♪. Do the same in 3/4 time, then in 4/4 time. Play each sequence.

Stop! Look! Play

Return to page 7.

Play the rhythmic patterns on treble C and middle C, RH and LH 3rd finger.

Count one measure and play.

| TREBLE G POSITION |

Find TREBLE G on the keyboard with RH 1st finger.

Play TREBLE G A B C D (RH 1 2 3 4 5)

Remember the G CLEF circles the line G ⟶

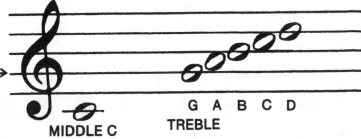

MIDDLE C   TREBLE

G A B C D

Using RH 1st finger, then LH 5th finger

1. Find the first note of Pattern No. 1 on the keyboard. (Treble G)

2. Look at the first note of Pattern No. 1 on the staff. (Treble G)

3. Play Pattern No. 1. STOP! Hold your finger on the last note.

4. WITHOUT LOOKING AT KEYBOARD OR FINGERS, play Pattern No. 2. STOP! Continue playing each pattern in the same way.

It is not necessary to play these in strict time. Take time to "picture" and "feel".

5. Return to Pattern No. 1. Say the names of the notes aloud.

6. Return to Pattern No. 1. Play and say the names of the notes as you play.

Daily Home Assignment: On the staff write your own 4 note pattern using the notes G, A, B, C, D. Use only 2nds and 3rds. Name the notes and <u>play each pattern</u>.

4THS

MIDDLE, TREBLE C

TREBLE G POSITIONS

Before you play

1. Look at the position and time signature.
2. Count one measure and play.

During the FIRST playing it is not necessary to play in strict time.

Taking time to "picture" and "feel" WITHOUT LOOKING AT THE KEYBOARD is very important!

Home Assignment: On the staff write one 4 measure musical example in 4/4 time beginning and ending
first on treble C, then middle C and treble G. Use 2nds, 3rds and many 4ths. Do the same in 3/4 time.
Name the notes and play each example.

See Appendix, UNIT ONE, "Stop! Listen!"

DESTINATION ONE

On your musical journey you have been introduced to:

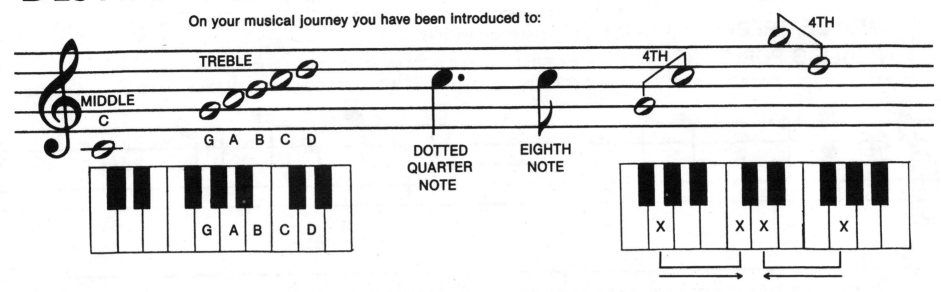

As you play the music in DESTINATION ONE.......REMEMBER

    1. Keep your eyes on the music! "See" the keyboard in your mind.

    2. Always look ahead as you play to see what is coming next!

Before you play

PREPARE

LOOK!   TELL WHAT YOU SEE!

Staff, time signature, note, hand and finger.

Count 1 measure and play. Be sure to accent the 1st and 3rd beat in $\frac{4}{4}$ time, or the 1st beat in $\frac{3}{4}$ time.

Love Somebody

Folk Song

Woodpecker's Song

Autumn Days

Jumping Jack

Trampoline Fun

1. Count 1 measure, then point and count.   (1 na 2 ta 3 ra 4 fa.)
2. Count 1 measure and play. Feel a steady, strong beat!

Where Have You Gone?

Hungarian Folk Song

Slavonic Dance

Hungarian Folk Song

1. Count 1 measure, then point and count. as you did on page 15.
2. Count 1 measure and play. Feel a steady, strong beat!

Gliding

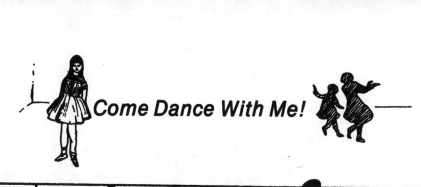

Come Dance With Me!

UNIT TWO

Stop! Look! Learn!

F CLEF

F CLEF

BASS STAFF

A staff with an F CLEF is called a BASS STAFF.

BASS G

The F CLEF is drawn with a dot beginning on this line F, and a dot above and below.

A note on the F line is played on the F below middle C.

F G MIDDLE C

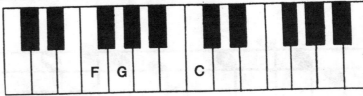

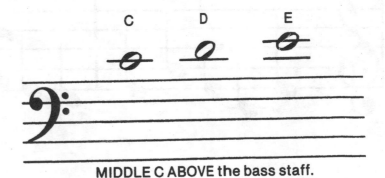

A note on the G space above F is played on the G below middle C.

LEDGER LINES

Notes above or below the staff are placed on short lines called ledger lines.

MIDDLE C BELOW the treble staff.

C B A

C D E

MIDDLE C ABOVE the bass staff.

TIME SIGNATURES

$$\frac{6}{8} \qquad \frac{3}{8}$$

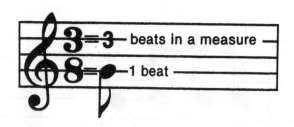

3 — 3 beats in a measure
8 — 1 beat

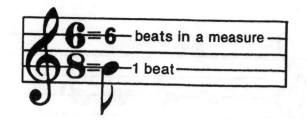

6 — 6 beats in a measure
8 — 1 beat

In $\frac{6}{8}$ time when the music is in a fast tempo, the ♪ are often connected in groups of 3.
Each group of 3 notes is counted as a beat.
So $\frac{6}{8}$ time may be counted in 6 or 2 beats depending on the tempo of the music.

1 2 3 4 5 6
1 na na 2 ta ta

1 2 3 4 5 6
1 na na 2 ta ta

1. Put the correct time signature at the beginning of each line of music.
2. Draw a line under each beat. ♩. _ _ _ ♩ _ ♪
3. In $\frac{6}{8}$ time: a) Write the beat numbers under the notes to show 6 beats in a measure.
   b) Write the beat numbers under the notes to show 2 beats in a measure.
4. Point to each ♪ as you count aloud. $\frac{3}{8}$ 1 2 3 $\frac{6}{8}$ 1 2 3 4 5 6 and 1 na na 2 ta ta.

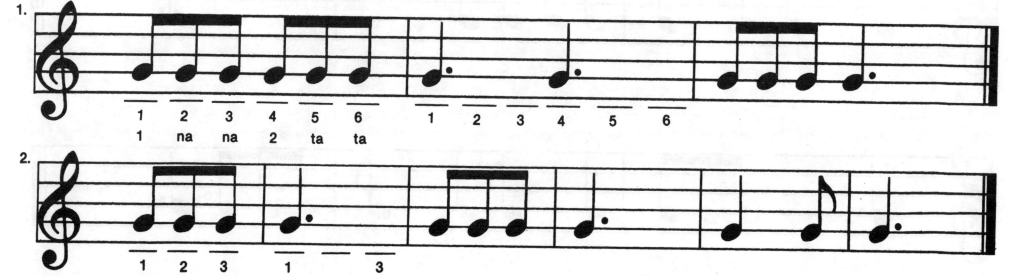

Stop! Look! Play!

Return to pages 21 and 22.

Play the rhythmic patterns on treble G, RH and LH 3rd finger.

Count one measure and play

BASS G POSITION

REMEMBER!

The F CLEF is drawn with a dot

beginning on this line F

and a dot above and below.

Find BASS G on the keyboard with left hand 5th finger.
Play BASS G A B C D. (LH 5 4 3 2 1)

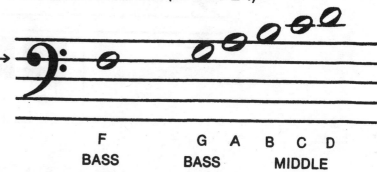

F
BASS

G A B C D
BASS MIDDLE

With LH 5th finger

1. Find the first note of Pattern No. 1 on the keyboard.
2. Look at the first note of Pattern No. 1 on the staff.
3. Play the patterns as you did in Treble G position on page 8.

4. Return to Pattern No. 1. Say the names of the notes aloud.
5. Return to Pattern No. 1. Play and say the names of the notes as you play.

Daily Home Assignment: On the staff write one different 4 note pattern in bass G position. Use 2nds, 3rds and 4ths. Name the notes and play each pattern.

See Appendix, UNIT TWO, "Stop! Listen"

DESTINATION TWO

On your musical journey since DESTINATION ONE you have been introduced to:

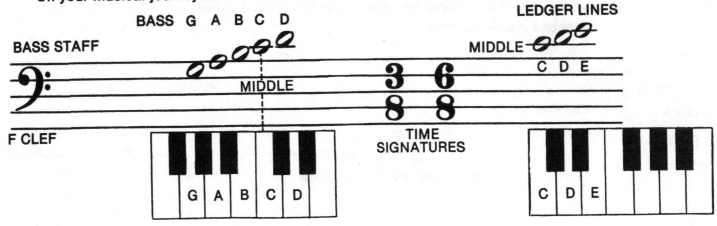

As you play the music in DESTINATION TWO........REMEMBER!

1. Keep your eyes on the music! "See" the keyboard in your mind.
2. Always look ahead as you play to see what is coming next!

Before you play
PREPARE

LOOK! TELL WHAT YOU SEE!

Staff, time signature, note, hand and finger.

Count 1 measure and play.

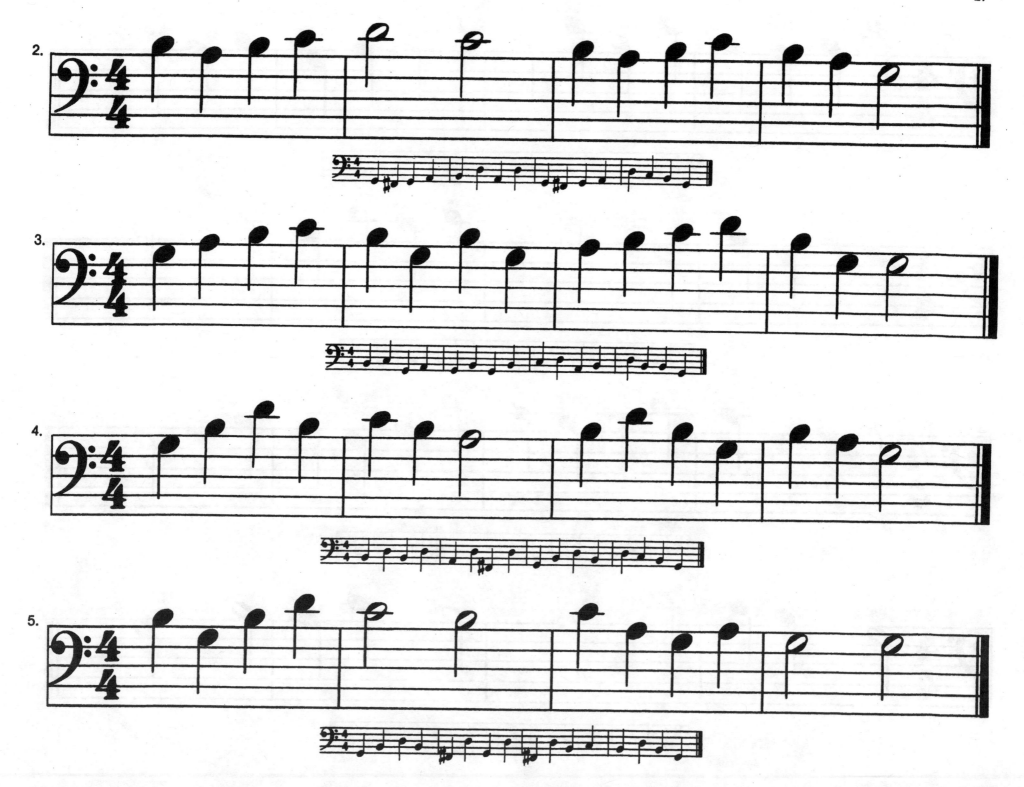

Taking Turns

Country Song

Taking Turns

Run and Jump

Joining Hands

Upstairs - Downstairs

Joining Hands

Merrily We Roll Along

Sleep, Baby, Sleep

Folk Song

UNIT THREE

Stop! Look! Learn!

INTERVAL of a 5TH

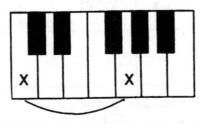

On the keyboard a 5TH looks like this.
Three keys are skipped.

On the staff a 5TH looks like this.
2 lines and 1 space or 2 spaces and 1 line are skipped.

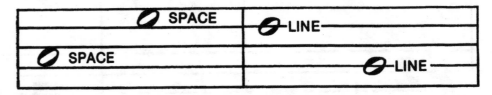

5TH UP   5TH DOWN

Put an X on the key a 5TH ABOVE each named key.
Connect the 2 keys.

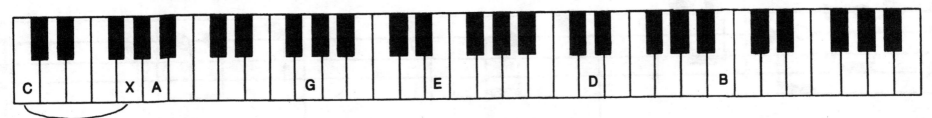

Draw a note on the line or space a 5TH ABOVE each note.

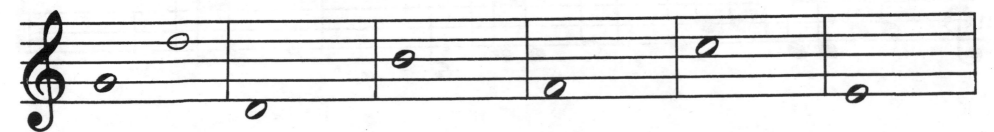

Put an X on the key a 5TH BELOW each named key. Connect the 2 keys.

Draw a note on the line or space a 5TH BELOW each note.

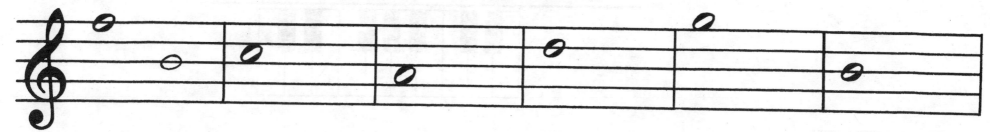

Connect and mark all the 5THS.

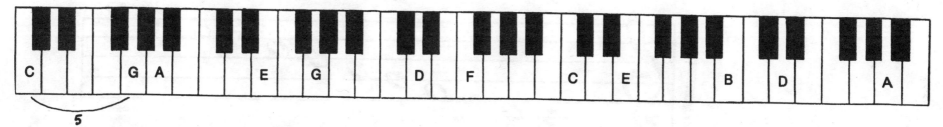

Connect and mark all the 5THS.

Daily Home Assignment: On the staff, draw a treble C, D, E, F, G and then the notes a 5th <u>BELOW</u> each one.
Now draw middle C, D, E, F, G adding the notes a 5th <u>ABOVE</u>. Draw treble G, A, B, C, D
with 5ths <u>BELOW</u>. Draw a bass clef, bass G, A, B, C, D and 5ths <u>BELOW</u>. Repeat assignments.
Name the notes and <u>play examples</u>.

NOTES on the BASS STAFF BASS C

A note on the BASS C space is played on the C BELOW MIDDLE C.

The GRAND STAFF

The TREBLE STAFF and BASS STAFF are connected to form the GRAND STAFF.

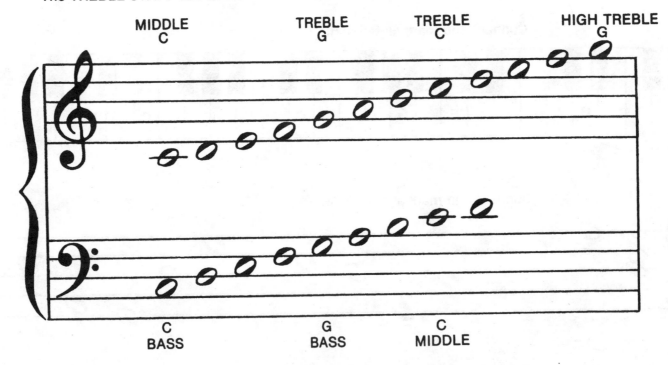

Daily Home Assignment: On Manuscript Paper draw a treble and bass clef to make a grand staff. Draw middle C, treble G and C, and high treble C on the treble staff. Draw bass C and G, and middle C on the bass staff. Write the name below each note.

Stop! Look! Play!

Return to page 38.

With your RH find and play all the Cs, then Ds, Es, Fs, Gs, As, and Bs on the TREBLE STAFF.

With your LH do the same on the BASS STAFF.

Find BASS C on the keyboard with RH 5th finger.

Play BASS C D E F G. (LH 5 4 3 2 1)

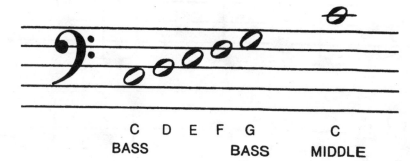

```
C    D  E  F  G         C
BASS           BASS   MIDDLE
```

BASS C
POSITION

With LH 5th finger

1. Find the first note of Pattern No. 1 on the keyboard.
2. Look at the first note of Pattern No. 1 on the staff.
3. Play the patterns as you did in Treble G position on page 8.

1.   2.   3.   4.

5.   6.   7.   8.

4. Return to Pattern No. 1. Say the names of the notes aloud.
5. Return to Pattern No. 1. Play and say the names of the notes as you play

Daily Home Assignment: On Manuscript Paper write one 4-note pattern in bass C position. Use 2nds, 3rds, 4ths and 5ths. Play the pattern and name the note.

42

5THS
MIDDLE, TREBLE C
TREBLE, BASS G
POSITIONS

Before you play

1. Look at the position and time signature.
2. Count one measure and play.

During the FIRST playing it is not necessary to play in strict time.

Taking time to "picture" and "feel" WITHOUT LOOKING AT THE KEYBOARD is very important!

Home Assignment: On the staff write one 4 measure musical example, in 𝄴 time, beginning and ending on treble C. Repeat this on middle C, bass C, treble G and bass G.
Do the same in 𝄵 time. Name the notes and play the examples.

See Appendix, UNIT THREE, "Stop! Listen!"

DESTINATION THREE

On your musical journey since DESTINATION TWO you have been introduced to:

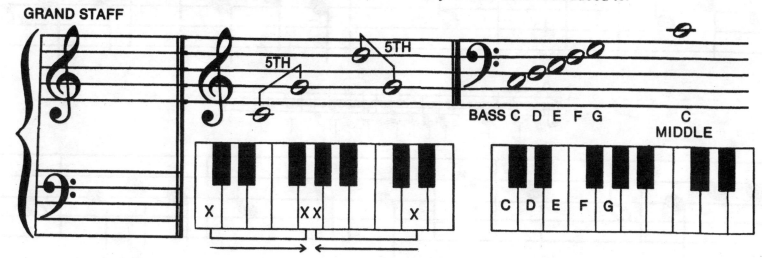

As you play the music in DESTINATION THREE........REMEMBER!

1. Keep your eyes on the music! "See" the keyboard in your mind.
2. Always look ahead as you play to see what is coming next!

Before you play
PREPARE

LOOK! TELL WHAT YOU SEE!

Staff, time signature, note, hand and finger.

Count one measure and play.

Snowfall

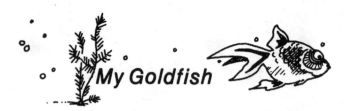

My Goldfish

Picnic Time

Swinging

Bugle Call

Puppet's Dance

Leap Frog

The Crocodile

Barcarolle

Offenbach

UNIT FOUR

Stop! Look! Learn!

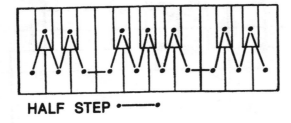

HALF STEPS

SHARP FLAT
NATURAL

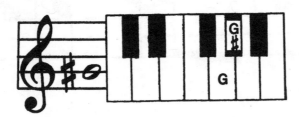

HALF STEP •————•

The distance between each key on the keyboard is called a HALF STEP.
Except for E-F and B-C, all half steps
are between a black key and a white key.
Each of the keys may be a ♯ or a ♭ , depending on the related note -
E♭may be D♯ , C♯may be D♭ .

This is a SHARP sign: ♯
If a SHARP is placed
in front of a note
the note is played
a HALF STEP ABOVE.

This is a FLAT sign: ♭
If a FLAT is placed
in front of a note
the note is played
a HALF STEP BELOW.

A. 1. Draw a ♯ in front of each note.
   2. Draw an arrow to the correct key on the keyboard.
   3. Write the name of the note in the blank below.
   4. Play and say the name of the note.

B. 1. Draw a ♭ in front of each note.
   2. Draw an arrow to the correct key on the keyboard.
   3. Write the name of the note in the blank below.
   4. Play and say the name of the note.

G♯

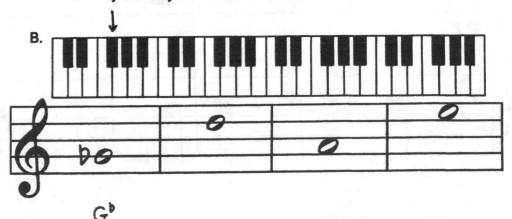

G♭

This is a NATURAL sign: ♮

If a NATURAL is placed in front of a note
the note is played as it "naturally" is,
WITHOUT a SHARP or FLAT.

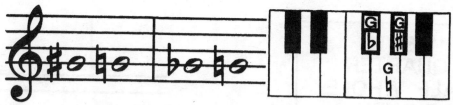

In each measure draw the same note with a ♯ in front of it.
Write the names of the notes in the blanks.
Play and say the names of the notes.

__F__ __F♯__ ____ ____ ____ ____

In each measure draw the same note with a ♭ in front of it.
Write the names of the notes in the blanks.
Play and say the names of the notes.

__B__ __B♭__ ____ ____ ____ ____

In each measure draw the same note with a ♮ in front of it.
Write the names of the notes in the blanks.
Play and say the names of the notes.

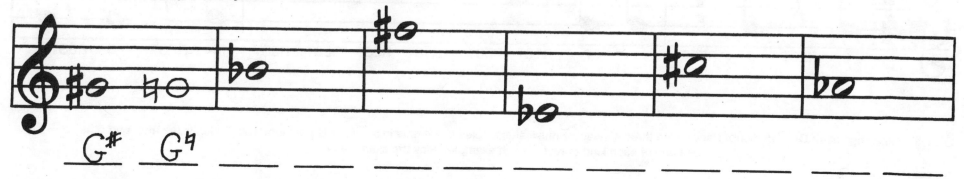

__G♯__ __G♮__ ____

**RESTS
QUARTER
HALF WHOLE
EIGHTH**

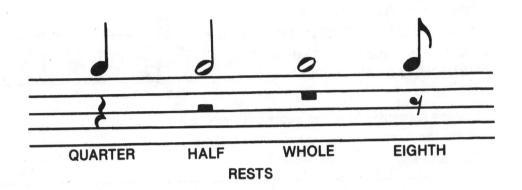

QUARTER   HALF   WHOLE   EIGHTH

RESTS

A REST is the sign of silence in music.

Silence for each rest lasts as long as its matching note would sound.

A whole rest may be used for a measure of silence in any time signature.

A. Point to each note as you count.

B. Point to each note and rest as you count,
but say "REST" instead of the number where there is a rest.
Draw the "matching" note in the blank under the rest.
Using RH 3rd finger, play, counting as above.

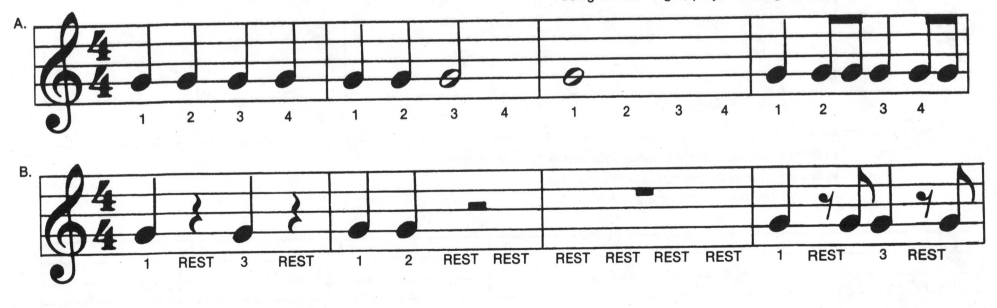

Home Assignment: On Manuscript Paper write three 4 measure musical examples in 4/4 time in any C or G position. Use 2nds, 3rds, 4ths, and 5ths.
Use one of each kind of rest in each example. Play the examples.

Stop! Look! Play!

Look at the staff, time signature, note, hand and finger. Count 1 measure and play.

58

Look at the staff, time signature, note, hand and finger. Count 1 measure and play.

See Appendix, UNIT FOUR, *"Stop! Listen!"*

DESTINATION FOUR

On your musical journey since DESTINATION THREE you have been introduced to:

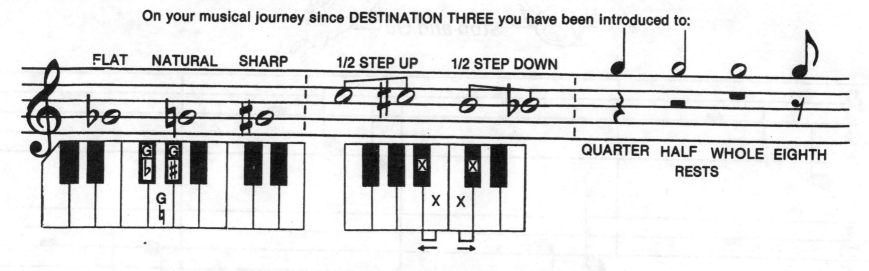

As you play the music in DESTINATION FOUR........REMEMBER!

1. Keep your eyes on the music! "See" the keyboard in your mind.

2. Always look ahead as you play to see what is coming next!

Before you play
PREPARE

LOOK!   TELL WHAT YOU SEE!

Staff, time signature, note, hand and finger.

Count 1 measure and play.

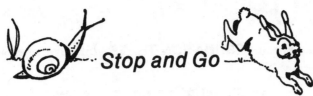

Stop and Go

Wiggly Worm

Halloween

Push  ups

The Robot

Twist and Turn

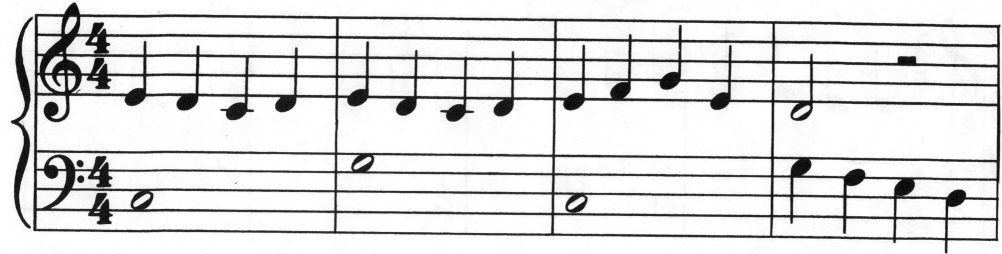

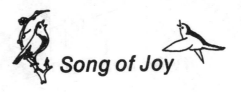 Song of Joy

Beethoven

Oats, Peas, Beans and Barley Grow

Folk Song

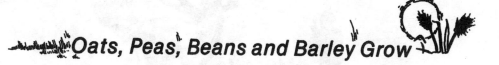

68

Musette

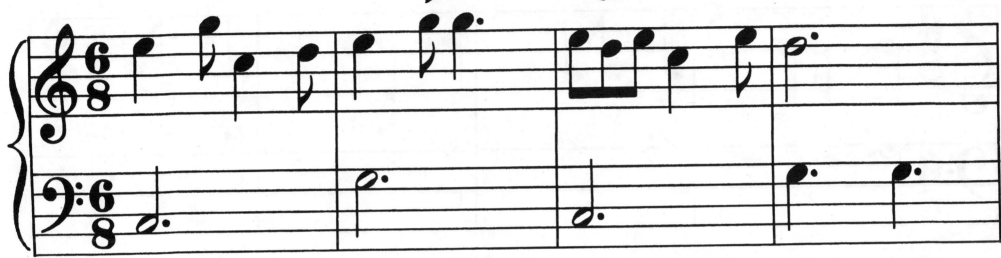

Jingle Bells

APPENDIX
Stop! Listen!

General Guidelines

1. All Preparations should be done with the student facing the piano, eyes open.

2. Unless otherwise specified, the student's eyes are to be closed during all listening exercises. This prevents distraction, allowing focus on listening.

3. Each listening exercise is to be done by the teacher at the lesson, with the parent continuing at home whenever possible. Persistent practice develops ability and confidence.

4. No negative comments or corrections such as "Wrong", or "That should have been" should be made. One of the strongest deterrents to any learning is the fear of making mistakes. If an incorrect answer is given, the teacher should go on with another example, then return. It may be necessary to do this more than once. Usually the answer will be correct after a few tries. If not, show the student what you played and give the answer. Do not specify that his answer was wrong. Focus on the right answer with no further comment.

5. Be sure that each exercise in a unit can be done with ease. It is necessary to be 100% successful in each step. Go on to the next exercise only when there is confidence and security.

6. Doing the so-called "optional" written work on manuscript paper is very important. Learning that is reinforced by playing, writing, and listening is absorbed and retained.

7. The metronome may be used to establish the beat and also during the playing of the rhythmic exercises.

UNIT ONE: Listening to 4ths in Middle and Treble C Positions

Preparation: Play C D E F G in both positions.
Play 4ths, C-F, D-G up, G-D, F-C down.
Ask student to sing these 4ths with note names as you play them.
(A 4th is heard in "Home On the Range")

Ex. A. Teacher: I will play C D E F G in middle and treble C positions, and then play 4ths in those positions.
Please tell me whether you heard 4ths in middle or treble C position.

Ex. B. Teacher: I will play 4ths, telling you the name of the first note.
Please tell me the name of the second note.
Open your eyes. Find and play both notes.

Review: Play and sing 2nds and 3rds in these positions. Repeat Ex. B with these intervals.

Ex. C. Teacher: I will play 2nds and 4ths telling you the name of the first note.
Please open your eyes, find and play the notes, name the interval and sing it with note names.

Ex. D. Teacher: (Same as Ex. C above, playing 3rds and 4ths).
(Ex. E should be done only after Ex. C and D can be done with ease.)

Ex. E. Teacher: (Same as Ex. C above, playing 2nds, 3rds and 4ths.)

Optional Work: Repeat Ex. B. Instead of answering orally or playing, the student draws the notes on Music Sheets.

Listening to Quarter and Eighth Notes.

Preparation: Establish a rhythmic beat ♩ = MM 72.
Clap the beat. Ask the student to clap with you.
Play and count 2 measures of quarter notes on a single repeated note.
1. Ask student to clap beat as you play.
2. Ask student to play quarters as you clap beat.
Play and count 2 measures of eighth notes.
1. Ask student to clap the beat as you play.
   Call attention to 2 notes per beat.
2. Ask student to play same eighth notes as you clap beat.

Ex. A. Teacher: I will tap a beat, then play.
Please tell me whether you hear quarter notes or eighth notes.

Suggested musical examples:

Ex. B. Teacher: I will tap a beat, then play.
Sometimes I will play quarter notes, sometimes eighth notes.
Please tell me when you hear quarter notes and when you hear eighth notes.

Suggested musical example:

Ex. C. Teacher: In this exercise you will play quarter notes and eighth notes.
Put your RH or LH 3rd finger on any key.
I will clap and count one measure of 4/4 time, then you will begin to play quarter notes.
Continue to play quarters until I say "Eighth notes", then without stopping, change from quarter to eighth notes.
Continue playing eighths until I say "Quarter notes", then without stopping, change to quarter notes again.
Repeat this exercise until changes can be made with ease.

Listening to Quarter, Dotted Quarter and Eighth Notes.

Preparation: Establish a rhythmic beat. ♩ = MM 72.
1. Clap the beat. Ask student to do this with you.
2. Play 2 measures of quarter notes, 4/4 time, counting as you play.
   Ask student to clap beat as you play.

3. Play 2 measures of dotted quarter and eighth notes, 4/4 time,
   counting as you play,
   "1 na 2 ta 3 ra 4 fa".
   Ask student to clap the beat as you play.

Ex. A. Teacher: I will tap the beat, then play.
Please tell me whether you hear quarter notes or dotted
quarter and eighth notes.

Suggested musical example:

Ex. B. Teacher: I will tap the beat, then play.
Please tell me when you hear quarters and when you hear
eighth notes.

Suggested musical example:

Ex. C. Teacher: In this exercise you will play dotted quarters, quarters and eighths.
Put your RH or LH 3rd finger on any key.
I will clap and count one measure of 4/4 time, then you will
begin to play quarter notes.
Continue to play quarters until I say "Dotted quarter and eighth
notes", then without stopping change.
Continue to play dotted quarters and eighths until I say
"Quarter notes", then without stopping change to quarter notes.
Repeat the exercise until changes can be made with ease.

Ex. D. Teacher: (Following the directions in Ex. C, use ♪ and ♩. ♪.)

UNIT TWO: Listening to 6/8 and 2/4 time

Preparation: Establish a rhythmic beat. (6/8, ♩ = MM 72, 2/4, ♩ = MM72)
Clap the beat. Ask the student to clap with you.
Play 4 measures of 6/8 time, eighth notes.
1. Ask student to listen to groups of 3 notes, or 3 small beats to
   each large one.
Play 4 measures of 2/4 time, eighth notes.
1. Ask student to listen to groups of 2 notes, or 2 small beats to
   each large one.
   (Point out that these are the half beats.)

Ex. A. Teacher: I will tap a beat, then play.
Please tell me whether you hear 6/8 or 2/4 time. You may clap the
eighth notes to feel whether there are 2 or 3 to each beat.

Suggested musical examples:

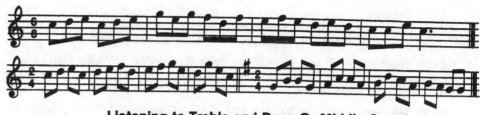

Listening to Treble and Bass G, Middle C and Treble C Positions

Preparation: Play middle and treble C positions, then bass and treble
G positions
Sing, point out location and relationship.

Ex. A. Teacher: I will play middle C, then CDEFG or GABCD. Please tell me which
position you hear: middle or treble C, bass or treble G.

Ex. B. Teacher: I will play one note, C or G, telling you it is C or G. Tell me
whether you hear middle or treble C, or treble or bass G.

Listening to 2nds in G Positions

Preparation: Play 2nds in both G positions, up and down. Sing with note
names.

Ex. A. Teacher: I will play 2nds in treble and bass G positions, telling you the
name of the first note.
Please tell me the name of the 2nd note.
Open your eyes. Play the notes you heard.

Listening to 3rds and 4ths in G Positions

Preparation: Play 3rds in both G positions, up and down. Sing with note names.

Ex. A. Teacher: (Follow the same procedure as in Ex. A above for 2nds, using
3rds, then 4ths.)

Optional Work: Repeat Ex. A above using 2nds, 3rds, 4ths. Instead of answering
orally, or playing, the student draws the notes on Music Sheets.

Review: Periodically return to Unit One, *Stop! Listen!*, Ex. B and Ex. C,
for reinforcement of rhythmic recognition, feeling and playing.

UNIT THREE: Listening to 5ths in Middle C, Treble C, Treble G, and Bass G Positions

Preparation: Play C D E F G (both positions)
Play C-G up, G-C down
Play G A B C D (both positions)
Play G-D up, D-G down
Ask student to sing these 5ths with note names as you play them.
(A 5th is heard in 'Twinkle, Twinkle Little Star')

Ex. A. Teacher: I will play middle C and treble C positions (CDEFG), then I will play the 5ths in those positions.
Please tell me if you hear middle or treble C position.

Ex. B. Teacher: I will play bass G and treble G positions (GABCD), then I will play the 5ths in those positions.
Please tell me if you hear bass or treble G position.

Ex. C. Teacher: I will play 2 notes, 5ths, (C-G, G-D up, G-C, D-G down) telling you the name of the first note.
1. Please tell me the name of the 2nd note.
2. Open your eyes. Find and play both notes.

Review: Before continuing, play and sing 2nds, then 3rds, and then 4ths in the G positions.

Ex. D. Teacher: I will play 2nds and 5ths in G positions, telling you the name of the first note.
Please open your eyes, find and play the notes, name the interval and sing it with note names.

Ex. E. Teacher: (Same as Ex. D above, with 3rds and 5ths)

Ex. F. Teacher: (Same as Ex. D above, with 4ths and 5ths)
(Ex. G should be done only after the preceding exercises can be done with ease.)

Ex. G. Teacher: (Same as Ex. D above, with 2nds, 3rds, 4ths, and 5ths)

Optional Work: Repeat Ex. C. Instead of answering orally or playing, draw the notes on manuscript paper.

UNIT FOUR: Listening to Half Steps - Sharps

Preparation: Play C-C♯ , D-D♯ , E-E♯ , F-F♯ , G-G♯ , in all three C positions, bass, middle, and treble.
Ask student to sing these half steps with sharp note names.
Play G-G♯ , A-A♯ , B-B♯ , C-C♯ , D-D♯ , in both G positions.
Ask student to sing these half steps with sharp note names.

Ex. A. Teacher: I will play two notes, telling you the name of the first note.
1. Please tell me the name of the second note.
2. Please open your eyes. Find and play both notes.

Listening to Half Steps - Flats

Preparation: 1. Play G-G♭ , F-F♭ , E-E♭ , D-D♭ , C-C♭ , in all three C positions.
Ask student to sing these half steps with flat note names.
2. Play D-D♭ , C-C♭ , B-B♭ , A-A♭ , G-G♭ , in both G positions.
Ask student to sing these half steps with flat note names.

Ex. A. Teacher: I will play two notes, telling you the name of the first note.
1. Please tell me the name of the second note.
2. Please open your eyes. Find and play both notes.

Optional Work: Repeat Ex. A of both parts of Unit Four. Instead of answering orally or playing, draw the notes on Manuscript Paper.